NEW TESTAMENT
REVELATIONS

GARY LEE GUERNSEY SR

WESTBOW
P R E S S
A DIVISION OF THOMAS NELSON

WestBow Press books may be ordered through booksellers or by contacting:

WestBow Press
A Division of Thomas Nelson
1663 Liberty Drive
Bloomington, IN 47403
www.westbowpress.com
1-(866) 928-1240

ISBN: 978-1-4497-3002-4 (sc)
Library of Congress Control Number: 2011919054

Printed in the United States of America

WestBow Press rev. date: 10/26/2011

CONTENTS

Jesus and Me

I was saved back in either 1969 or 1970. I was saved and attended a church where the pastor really rooted and grounded me in the Lord Jesus Christ, thank God. From the time I was saved, I started reading the Bible daily. I mostly read the New Testament and not too much of the Old. I did not really understand why the New Testament was of such interest to me at that time, but I do now. I would read from Matthew to Revelations, a chapter a day, and sometimes much more than that.

After about five years, the pastor left the church and things started to change. The new pastors were not nearly as zealous of Jesus as I was, so I started looking for another church—one that put Jesus first and foremost. My wife, though, was happy at the same old church and kept attending. I finally was unable to find a church and started drifting back into the world and getting ahead in the world, feeling the church had let me down. I could not understand why others did not see Jesus the way I did. So I went back into the world feeling I had been let down by man, not by Jesus.

Though I had drifted from my Lord, He had never left me, just as He had promised He would not. I still maintained my belief in my Lord. I just wasn't following Him like I should have been. I stayed that way from 1973 to 2003. In 1983, we moved as a family from Cadillac, Michigan, to Fort Pierce, Florida. I worked in a body shop there for three years. From there we moved to Hollywood, Florida, for twelve years while our children were growing up. Three of them moved north to South Carolina where their uncle, my wife's brother, lived and started working there. My one son stayed in south Florida (is still there), but my wife and I moved from Florida in 1998 to Rock Hill, South Carolina, where my other three children lived.

It was a simple move for my wife and me, and I transferred with my company, Winn Dixie. I worked in North Carolina as a body man at the Winn Dixie Center, same as I did in Florida. Finally after a number of things happened in our lives, I went back to my Lord in 2003. I was "down and out" you might say.

When I felt the Lord strongly drawing me, I said to Him: "Lord, I want to be real, and I want to understand You and Your Word so I can explain it to others and make them understand." In my religious life in the past, I felt that a lot of things were not well understood, but rather just accepted because that was the way it was. When I turned back to Jesus in 2003, I found Him still there for me and by me, as He never left nor forsook me.

This time my Jesus brought me back in a mighty way, a very powerful way. I started to read the New Testament again day after day, and the Lord started dealing with me. Draw close to Him and He will draw close to you. The Lord started to deal with me on sin and disobedience, which are the same. He showed me that obedience was righteousness for us and that believing and accepting His Word is of utmost importance. From that point on, things started to get pretty heavy in the Word. The Lord would show me things and make me to understand them so that I was able to explain them to others. I found things I had read before in His word, but I never saw or understood them in this manner. I soon learned (as my Lord showed me) that this was not just about Jesus but was ALL about Jesus. I was finally back where I felt I belonged with my Lord. My Lord pulled me back in a mighty way to Him, and I soon learned that it would come with a cost. However, this time I had weighed the cost of being back with Jesus as before; I had let man let me down and not my Lord.

Soon I found that what Jesus was showing me was quite contrary to many churches' doctrines and beliefs. I did not let this stop me and continued to pursue the Lord and His word with understanding. The Lord showed me that the New Testament was my (and others') eternal life assurance policy. Soon the revelations that I was receiving were coming at me very quickly. These revelations, though, were not always accepted by other Christians. Christians seem to have a way of believing what they have been taught rather than what you might show them. The Word of God became the top priority in my life, and those who knew me would tell you that I had really changed. My own family members found it hard to understand me. The Word of God was changing my whole life and everyone that knew me knew I was a new creature. I was unable to keep my mouth closed about the word of God and what He had shown me.

My daughter-in-law told me she did not really like me now the way I had changed. I told her that I could remember that she did not like the way I was before either. I told her that makes me wonder if she ever did like me at all. God's wisdom started to work though and by His word that I was learning.

My wife and I were in a pharmacy in Greenville, South Carolina, to pick up my prescription that I had had for a number of months. The woman at the counter told me that the prescription would be $190.00. I told her there had to be a mistake. She checked and said that there was no mistake; my wife's insurance had apparently changed. I was very disgusted, but "Be ye angry, and sin not," the Word says (Ephesians 4:26). So I said to her, "Well, I'm glad to see that there is still love in the world." She immediately nodded her head in agreement, and I said, "Even if it is the love of money." Her face really changed. Needless to say, she had no comment. Now with God's Word being placed in me, I was beginning to see the iniquity that was in the world.

I sometimes would speak out against this iniquity to others and would make my wife angry with me. She would say, "You're not going to change things by doing that." No, but it made me feel better. Jesus in John 7:7 told his brothers, who did not understand Him, "The world cannot hate you; but me it hateth, because I testify of it, that the works thereof are evil." The world does not like to be told it is doing evil. And the world will hate you as Jesus said. I often tell people that Jesus was not so much crucified for what He did as for what He said. This is what the religious leaders of that day did not like.

Christians should speak out against wrong doings. This is part of the job we are called to do. We should hate iniquity and not hate those who commit the iniquity. As Christians we should hate the sin, but not the sinner. Jesus came to save the world and not condemn it. We must separate the sin from the sinner. It is our job to love the sinner but not the sin.

I soon found that what my Lord had shown me by His Word was not the common view that was shared by others on the same matters or scriptures. I was careful to establish a belief I had been given on two or three scriptures in the New Testament. Even though I was shown things in the Old

Testament, they would be in complete agreement with the New Testament. The Lord showed me that in the mouth of two or three witnesses shall something be established.

One church I had been attending for almost a year had a man in that church that told me I had a demon because of the way I explained the scriptures to him. I smiled and said: "They said the same thing about my Lord." Jesus said that if they have called the master of the house Beelzebub how much more would they call them of his household. I was seeing scriptures come to pass in front of my very eyes, just as Jesus said it would be. I soon found that what Jesus said was also about me.

In Matthew 10:34-6, Jesus said: "Think not that I am come to send peace on earth: I came not to send peace but a sword. For I am come to set a man at variance against his father, and the daughter against her mother; daughter-in-law against her mother-in-law. And a man's foes shall be they of his own household." I saw this happen with my very eyes with not only members of my family but members of the household of God also. Surprised? Yes. Hurt? Yes somewhat, but not altogether. Amazed? Yes, I was. I soon was shown that the ministry of my Lord and His gospel was no cotton candy ministry. Forget the sugar as it was most of the time not very sweet. I soon saw that men did hate me because of what I believed of the Word, and they would not see or rather refused to see. God never shows anyone anything when they have a closed mind and a hardened heart. These two things God has a hard time getting through. It took me 20 years of time to get rid of what man had tried to drive into my mind about the Word of God. I consider that what I was being put through was a small thing compared to what my Lord went through for me. I have no regrets at all. I did find that when God shows you something that you may not receive more until you share what you have been shown with others, regardless of how they may feel about you and what you believe. It sure seems that the more revelation of the Word I received that the tougher the battle became. My Lord would sometimes throw me into the ring bear fisted and say, "Show them My word."

The battles may have been tough, yet not all would refuse the word. Some would see what I had been shown. I tell people, "I can show you something in the Word of God, but unless the Holy Spirit reveals it to you, you will never see it." In John 16:13, Jesus said: "Howbeit when he, the spirit of truth is come, He will guide you into all truth." This was happening to me. The truth of God's Word was now being shown to me, and it was nothing like I had seen or understood before.

Some people say that the Holy Spirit *leads* you into all truth. This is one of the misquotations of God's word I find most often. The Spirit *guides* us and does not lead us. If we believe the guidance of the Spirit and follow that guidance, then the Spirit becomes our leader but not until we follow the guidance many times. Sometimes when the Spirit is guiding us to a truth of God's Word, we will not follow that guidance because of wrong teaching; and we miss out on what we are supposed to see -- what God would have us to know and believe. With the Word of the God and the guidance of the Holy Spirit, we are given all the tools we need. We must open our hearts and minds to His Word of truth. My spiritual growth has seemed to me to be very fast and very complete in understanding. The Word says, "The Comforter… will…bring all things to your remembrance, whatsoever I have said unto you" (John 14:16).

First, we must read the words of Jesus before the Spirit can bring them to our minds. I have heard so many people tell me. I just want to be used of God. God is a God of His Word. To know God and His will is to know His Word. Sometimes we hinder the use of the God in our lives because we do not know His Word or don't use it when we are supposed to. Once the Word enters our hearts and minds, then things will start to happen. The Word says, "Out of the abundance of the heart the mouth speaketh" (Matthew 12:34). The more Word we get in us, the more Word that comes out of us. The Word is true and it does happen just like it says.

I tried so hard to witness to others after I had come back to Jesus, and it seemed like I was not doing anything for my Lord. One day, Jesus said to me, "Lee, (He does call me by my name) you are working too hard at this. You need to sow my Word and let it do its perfect work, that's what it is supposed to do." When I followed what Jesus said, I would see things happen; and I knew that I was doing what I was supposed to. Each and every time I read God's Word, the Word enters my heart and I mediate on His Word at night or during the day. This is when My Lord has shown me what He would have me to see. God does not always show me an entire thing all at once. Sometimes He will show me something in His Word, but not all of it. I have had it take years before I have received the complete vision. This may well be my fault; I am so eager to see what my Lord has for me and others that I fail to see something my Lord may be trying to show me. Thank you, Lord, for being such a patient God. Romans 10:17: "So then faith cometh by hearing, and hearing by the Word of God." So the more I read the Word of God, believe, and get it in me, the more pleasing it is to God. Hebrews 11:6, "But without faith it is impossible to please Him [God]." I believe in Matthew 3:17, when God said: "This is my Beloved Son, in whom I am well pleased." God was well pleased in Jesus because of His great faith He had in the Father.

God has been so good in teaching me His Word, especially since in school I was a hard learner. The longer

I serve my Lord, though, the more I find the less I know. God is not a respecter of persons, and whatever time we give Him in study or reading of His Word will be well repaid to us in knowledge and understanding. By knowing His Word I have learned to know my Lord much better. We have a relationship that the world does not nor cannot understand. I am not Jesus only, but I am Jesus first and Jesus foremost. Many of you that read this book may have already heard or seen in God's Word what I write about. I have had one man explain something that God had shown Him in the Word and found it was exactly what I had been shown although the roads that were taken to get to the revelation were somewhat different. I found that what was seen by the both of us was the very same. God is so amazing! His ways are beyond finding out. Though *how* we had been shown was different, *what* we had been shown was the very same. The Word says there is nothing new under the sun. I myself am not a very good man for praying to my Lord. I don't always know what to say or how to say it, but one thing I am is a good listener to my Lord.

Signs Following

One of the signs in Mark 16:17 that Jesus said would follow those who believe in Him is that they shall speak with New Tongues. Though there have been other signs that follow the believer, this particular one has been clearly shown to me by God's Word. There are numerous other scriptures in the Word that will give more meaning to this particular scripture. I am not a sign follower of the Word, but I do strongly believe in the sign of New Tongues.

According to *Strong's Concordance*, #2537 *Kainos* means **new** (especially in freshness) while #3501 the word *new* is referring to age. So *Kainos* –"*new*" (#2537) is the word used in the New Testament. Now the other tongues that were spoken of on the day of Pentecost are not a **new** tongue but are rather other and also numerous tongues (languages) that were spoken at the outpouring of the Holy Spirit.

The New Tongues are a sign of being a believer in the Lord Jesus Christ. Mark 16:17: "And these signs shall follow them that believe; ... they shall speak with new tongues." Jesus was saying that believers in Him would speak, prophesy (i.e. speak under inspiration) in the words of the New Testament. Since I have been saved, I have been especially drawn to the New Testament even though I believe in both the New and Old Testaments. My salvation as a Gentile starts in the New while the Old is primarily about God's people, the Jews. In Matthew 7:21-22 Jesus says: "Not every one that saith unto me, Lord, Lord, shall enter into the kingdom of heaven: but he that doeth the will of my father which is in heaven. Many will say to me in that day, Lord, Lord, have we not prophesied in thy name? and in thy name have cast out devils? And in thy name done many wonderful works?" If you will take this scripture and compare it to Mark 16, you will find that this person in Matthew 7 was using the signs of a believer here in talking to the Lord. The "prophesied in thy name" is to speak with New Tongues. "In thy name cast out devils" is also a sign and also are the many wonderful works. Therefore, this person was saying, "Lord, I am a believer in you" by these signs he had stated. So the New Tongues are for a sign of a believer.

What about the other tongues in Acts 2? The Apostle Paul gives a very clear cut understanding on other tongues in I Corinthians 14:20-22: "Brethren, be not children in understanding: howbeit in malice be ye children, but in understanding be men. In the law it is written, With men of other tongues and other lips will I speak unto this people; and yet for all that will they not hear me, saith the Lord. Wherefore tongues are for sign, not to them that believe, but to them that believe not; but prophesying serveth not for them that believe not, but for them which believe." So here Paul tells us that the other tongues were a sign for non-believers while prophesying (speaking in a New Tongue) is for the believer.

Now I do believe that after the day of Pentecost the other tongues are a gift of the Holy Spirit and are for self-edification, unless there is an interpreter in the midst while the other tongues are being used. So it would sound to me like things are a little turned around here. My wife and I were saved in a Pentecostal church. This church believed if you did not speak in tongues, then you had not received the Holy Spirit. However, I Corinthians 12:8-11 tells of many spiritual gifts. The Apostle Paul warns us not to be children in understanding on this matter (I Cor.14:20).

Please know that my reading and studying of the New Testament is based on five books only: the King James Bible is the first, the *Strongs Exhaustive Concordance of the Bible* (King James), Thayer's Lexicons (one Old Testament and one New), and a Webster's dictionary. Anything that is revealed to me I truly feel is of my Lord because I do not read any other books on the Bible at all so that I do not cloud my mind with what someone else may say. This gives my Lord free reign to show me what He will. I also participate in Bible studies with other brothers who have provoked me to deeper thinking.

IN THE BEGINNING

In Genesis 1, the Word of God says: "God created the heaven and the earth." The word *create* in Hebrew (#1254 in *Strongs*) means "to create, to produce, to polish, hence to fashion." Though the earth and heavens had been created by God, they were without form, Gen. 1:2. So God first *creates* and then He *forms*.

In the 1980s, my wife, children, and I, visited my brother–in-law in Detroit, Michigan. He took me to the Pontiac Motor Division plant where his father-in-law worked as a designer. His job was to take the ideas he was given and draw them on paper in detail. This was creating something from man's ideas. It was the first step to take place before the auto was formed by the materials used in the forming process. Man was created in the likeness of his Creator—God--so we have the likeness of Him. Man will first create something on paper and then usually out of another material before it is actually formed into being. God creates, then forms. Gen. 1:27: "So God created man in his own image, in the image of God created he him; male and female created he them." Genesis 2:7: "And the Lord God formed man of the dust of the ground, and breathed into his nostrils the breath of life, and man became a living soul." This is when man came into existence in the world. The word *form* (Strong's #3335) means "To form, fashion as a potter does." So in the beginning man was created in God's image and likeness, but in Genesis we see that word *form* is stressed here in the creation of man.

What is the "image of God" and "likeness of God"? Man offers many answers, but what does God's Word say? Romans 1:23 says, "And changed the glory of the uncorruptible God into an image make like to corruptible man, and to birds, and fourfooted beasts, and creeping things." Therefore, man is now corruptible after having sinned. He was not before sinning because he had God's image, Who is incorruptible. In Corinthians, Paul gives us a more explanation. I Corinthians 15:52-3: "In a moment, in the twinkling of an eye, at the last trump: for the trumpet shall sound, and the dead shall be raised incorruptible and we shall be changed. For this corruptible must put on incorruption, and this mortal must put on immortality." So this sounds like we will be changed back into the image of God in which we were first created.

Want more proof? Genesis 5:1: "This is the book of the generations of Adam. In the day that God created man, in the likeness of God made he him." No more *image* here. Why? This is after Adam sinned and had lost the image of God. The image of God was gone when man sinned. Man became mortal, corruptible and had sin, which caused all of it. When I saw this, it made me so thankful for my Lord Jesus. Through Him and by Him we regain the image of our Creator in the resurrection. Jesus is the image of God, without sin (Colossians 1:15 and II Corinthians 4:4). Because of Jesus my Lord and my faith in Him, I can one day have the image of God once more as I should have had in the beginning. Thank you, Jesus!

Evening and Morning

The second thing that God created after the heaven and the earth: light. Genesis 1:3: "Let there be light: and there was light." Note that on the fourth day God created a light for day and for the night. Genesis 1:16-19: "And God made two great lights; the greater light to rule the day, and the lesser light to rule the night: he made the stars also. And God set them in the firmament of the heaven to give light upon the earth. And to rule over the day and over the night, and to divide the light from the darkness: and God saw that it was good. And the evening and the morning were the fourth day."

I believe that when God said "Let there be light" in Genesis 1:3 this is when Jesus entered the world. In John 8:12 Jesus says that He is the light of the world. Colossians 1:16 says "All things were created by Him." Hebrews 1:2 says the worlds were made by Him. Without Jesus there could not have been any life because God has made Jesus to be life for us. This is why Jesus is the One we should come to know in this short span of life we have been given. If we leave this world not knowing Jesus, then there is no more life for us. He is our only hope of eternal life after this life.

In II Corinthians 4:6 says: "For God, who commanded the light to shine out of darkness...." God's Word is true, and we see that when Jesus, the light of the world, was born at night the light shined out of darkness. The shepherds came to Jesus by night. The wise men followed the star and came to Jesus by night. Nicodemus came to Jesus by night. It became dark in the Jesus' last hours on the cross. I don't think all these nighttime things were accidental. The light did shine out of darkness as the Word says. So once God had brought light into the world, He then created life here on earth. Genesis 1:4-5 says: "And God saw the light, that it was good: and God divided the light from the darkness. And God called the light Day, and the darkness he called Night. And the evening and the morning were the first day." So God called the light day, and God called the darkness night."

Now if we look at this carefully in the Word -- day, light, darkness, and night -- we should be able to see that God's day had no darkness at all in it, for day is light. Now look at the Word: "the evening and the morning were the first day." What is there about the evening and the morning that the Word states here? Well, the evening is when the sun sets, and the morning is when the sun rises. So this tells me that that God's day consisted of nothing but light as light is day and darkness night.

I John 1:5: "This then is the message which we have heard of him, and declare unto you, that God is light, and in Him is no darkness at all." In John 11:9 Jesus asked, "Are there not twelve hours in the day?" Jesus is indicating *day* here is light only. The day which we talk of as a twenty-four hour day is told only to be twelve hours, which is a half day and is only daylight.

Why does God's Word say the evening and the morning were the first day then? Why did it not say the morning (when the sun rises and the evening (when the sun sets) were the first day. This is the way we say it and understand it, right? Well, this is God's Word and God calls the last first and the first last. This is the way of God and that is exactly how He says it in His Word. Also Mark 10:31 and Luke 13:30 tell us this.

Now let's go back to the word *day* as used in God's Word. This word is very interesting in other ways. We look at the 24 hour day in man's calculations as this is how we understand it and have been taught this. But how does God see it? II Peter 3:8 helps us: "But, beloved, be not ignorant of this one thing, that one day is with the Lord as a thousand years, and a thousand years as one day." So God's timetable tells me that God sees a day to be one thousand years, not 24 hours. With that thought in mind, let's look at what God told Adam. In Genesis 2:17 God said that if Adam ate of the tree of knowledge he "would surely die." So Adam was supposed to die within 24 hours? No, he was to die within one thousand years. How long did Adam live? Genesis 5:5: "And all the days that Adam lived were nine hundred and thirty years: and he died." Did he die in the same day as he ate of the tree? Yes, he died within the one thousand years which is God's day, not man's.

With this in mind, when Jesus came to earth and was born of Mary, most claim it to have been four thousand years after Adam. Well, now it is two thousand years after Jesus. If we take four thousand and two thousand, then we are now in the sixth day of God's timetable here on earth. Jesus will come again in the last day, which will be the last thousand years of earth's life. So if we are now in the last part of the sixth day, that means we are getting ready to enter the seventh or last day really soon. Come quickly, Lord Jesus! He shall appear to those who look for Him. I am looking for Him any time now!

Referring to time, Jesus says "last days" and refers to the "last day." If a day is a thousand years and a thousand years as a day with God, then we are now in the end of the six thousand years of the existence of man. If this is the proper view, then we are in the last days and will soon enter the last day (or seven thousandth year) of our earth. In John 6:39-40 Jesus speaks of raising up in the last day all that the Father had given Him. This resurrection, the first, is spoken of in Revelations 20:4-6, which is the last day, when the saints are raised up first. So the Word says that we, the saints, shall be judged first. I Peter 4:17: "For the time is come that judgment must begin at the house of God; and if it first begin at us, what shall the end be of them that obey not the gospel of God?" So everyone must die, and then be judged. Hebrews 9:27: "It is appointed unto men once to die, but after this the judgment." So first we die, are resurrected, or raptured, and then we are judged, even the saints. Romans 14:10 and II Corinthians 5:10 tell us: "For we shall all stand before the judgment seat of Christ" to answer. Those who think that because you are saved you won't then be judged, well the Word does not say that anywhere. This judgment of Christ is also spoken of in Revelations 20:4-15. These verses speak of both judgments: the judgment seat of Christ first, then the White Throne Judgment one thousand years later. The disciples who were with Christ here on earth are those in verse 4 that sat upon the thrones as Jesus said they would in Matthew 19:28 and Luke 22:30. All these scriptures come together in the Word of God.

CHRISTMAS TIME

Around the holiday season we see many things that decorate and remind us that Christmas season is upon us once more. I love this time of year. Sometimes I wish the Christmas spirit would last all year long. Many things are being done and said to try to take Christ out of Christmas. This lets me know that the Devil is working really hard because he knows his time is short. Christmas has become so commercial to generate money, and somehow robs us Christians of the Spirit of Christmas.

One day, a week or two before Christmas, I was on my way into town and saw a sign in front of a Baptist church with these words:

"Jesus is the Reason for the Season."

As I thought on this something came to mind, and I could not wait to get home and write it down. This is it:

"Jesus is the reason for the season." This is No L.

"Jesus is the real Son for the seal son" (With the L)

Maybe this is one more sign of the times that we are to know about.

Read about the seals in Revelation 5 and 6.

GOD IS ALL POWERFUL

One day as I pondered Colossians 1:16, something happened. Colossians 1:16: "For by him were all things created, that are in heaven, and that are in earth, visible and invisible, whether they be thrones, or dominions, or principalities, or powers: all things were created by him, and for him." And then I thought about the word *power*. Then I heard the Lord say to me: "Lee, if I am all powerful, then why do I need ***powers***?" This made me really think.

The Bible says that man was created in God's image and likeness. We lost the image to sin, but we still retain the likeness of God. This means we are like our God in many ways. One way man is like God is our desire to create laws to maintain order. God has done this in our universe. Most scientists, even atheists, will admit that the planets and the whole universe are held in place and order is maintained by the law of gravity. Now if one of these gravitational laws is broken for any reason, then the universe goes out of order and strange things happen.

We, like God, have the ability to create other powers. For instance, we can move dirt with a shovel. When we want a lot of dirt moved in a hurry, we have other things man has created to do this job very quickly and very easily. Many other powers man has created to assist him in his ventures. When a lawmaker, a politician, makes a law of the land, then it is passed and goes on the books—becomes a law. Now the politician does not police the law, but turns it over to another power to make sure the law is kept. Let's say that one breaks a law and is caught by the police, then what? One goes to the judge who will convict one of his lawlessness and punish him for breaking the law.

Man, then, creates many powers in this world and it all comes from our likeness of God. I believe that once God makes a law that all the powers He has created in the universe go into work to make sure His Word is kept. I believe that creation knows its Creator and Who He is. So if and when God's laws are not obeyed, then His created powers go to work. The old saying, "God will get you for that," comes from a lack of knowledge. God does not "get you for that" but rather the created powers of God work to make sure His Word or law is kept. When we break a law and are caught by a policeman or other law enforcement, then we can't say, "Well, it was the Lawmaker's fault." You see when God does something, it is perfect and the powers help to keep it that way. When God created Adam and Eve, he was and she was, perfect in all ways. Only once man sinned did things go out of God's order. Disobeying God's Word, or laws, is sin. This is the only thing I have found that will take something out of God's order that He put it in. Look around us today. We see many things happening that are not normal, that are unusual one might say. Well, something tells me that sin is starting to abound more and more in this world.

Whenever I see numerous tornadoes, numerous earthquakes, and numerous other weather phenomena, I know that at the very pit of it is man's unrepented sin. So don't blame God when you see the out of order happenings; blame man and his love of sin and darkness. The Word says God is good and that all good things come from above. God goes by the same rules He gives us to go by. Matthew 7:17-18 and 20: "Even so every good tree bringeth forth good fruit; but a corrupt tree bringeth forth evil fruit. A good tree cannot bring forth evil fruit; neither can a corrupt tree bring forth good fruit…. Wherefore by their fruits ye shall know them." God does not pretend to be both good and evil. This is a man-made thing. When something is bad (or evil) it came from the accuser, the great deceiver himself, who works hard to get people to believe it. The only reason one says something like this is a lack of knowledge. Satan will take full advantage of a lack of knowledge.

God is good and the Devil is evil. We need to start putting blame for wrongdoing on the One to Whom it belongs. So the next time you see something out of order or that normally does not happen, point the finger at man's sin and the great deceiver, knowing that these two work together with one another.

Marriage

When it comes to marriage, one may find a lot of different views. What does God's Word really say about marriage and divorce? Well, we have to look in the New Testament for these answers. The Old Testament and Moses' law were not as clear on these matters.

In the Gospel of Mark 10:2, the Pharisees confront Jesus on this matter, tempting Him. Note that when they asked Jesus the question, "Is it lawful for a man to put away his wife?" Jesus threw the ball back into their court, for He knew their thoughts. Jesus asked them, "What did Moses command you?" (Mark 10:3) Jesus knew that they would honor Moses and what he said, but they would not honor Jesus for they were looking to accuse Him to the leaders. They said, "Moses suffered to write a bill of divorcement, and to put her away. And Jesus answered and said unto them, 'For the hardness of your heart he wrote you this precept'" (Mark 10:4-5). The word *precept* in *Strong's Concordance* is #1785 and means "injunction, an authoritative prescription." We see in Matthew 19 the same story but with a little added. In Matthew 19:8 Jesus says, "But from the beginning it [divorce] was not so." So this means that Moses allowed divorce because the Jews would not accept God's law on this matter. So we see here that divorce is not of God, but was allowed by Moses, whom the Jews recognized as an authority.

Jesus' final word on the matter is in Mark 10:11-12: "And He saith onto them, 'Whosoever shall put away his wife, and marry another, committeth adultery against her. And if a woman shall put away her husband, and be married to another, she committeth adultery." This is quite the opposite in today's world and the way things are taught.

Marriage in today's' world is something that carries very little honor and is something that people enter into lightly and get out of quickly if need be. I know not everyone feels this way; but for the most part, the world does and really has no place here for God's laws. At one a time (I am unable to pin this time down although I have checked) the marriage ceremony was performed by only a pastor or priest of the church. South Carolina, which has a divorce law, had no record in the library stating when this stopped and marriage became a thing that a Justice of the Peace (or just about anyone licensed by the state) could perform. My own belief on this matter is that at one time a very wealthy man divorced his wife, which was probably not permitted by the churches at that time. Of course, this probably would have been a divorce that would have been honored by the state he lived in at that time, as money buys almost anything. Once divorced, this wealthy man sought to remarry another woman and found that no church would perform the ceremony; so somehow with his money and influence, he got the laws changed in the state so that it was legal in the state anyway. I have no record of how this was done, but it seems a reasonable theory.

So now through the years, we see what the common acceptance of marriage is, at least according to most states. In Mark 7:1-13 is a story of how man's traditions will come to make the law of God of no effect. This is much the same way that marriage has become. Once it was an honorable thing that was only done by the churches, or I should say, only allowed by the churches. Nowadays man's tradition and money, big money, have made God's law of no effect, as Jesus said.

I know that there are some who will say, "Yes, but for the cause of fornication, one can divorce as the Bible says." Well, let's talk about this matter and what God's Word says about it. The book of Matthew is the only place where this will be found. Matthew, the author whose name was also Levi, was one of the twelve apostles. Most believe Matthew was written primarily to the Jews. The view is confirmed by the fact that there are about sixty references to the Jewish prophecies and about forty quotations from the Old Testament. Also some of the Jewish customs and traditions are shown here.

Let's start at Matthew 1. Here we have the genealogy of Jesus. In verse 18, we see how the birth of Jesus occurred, at least in Joseph's eyes at that time. Note in verse 18 that Joseph and Mary were espoused, or engaged, to each other. In a Jewish engagement, one had to take a vow, much the same as the marriage vow, but a little different. This vow was to show that you were promised to each other and no one else for marriage. While engaged then, the man and woman were known as husband and wife. In verse 19, Joseph is called Mary's husband even though they were not yet married. This is also stated in Luke 2:5 where Mary is called Joseph's "espoused wife." So once engaged, they were known by Jewish law to be husband and wife. Also once engaged, the couple could only separate by a divorce. Yes, a written statement of divorce was the only way to break an engagement under Jewish law.

In Matthew 1:18, Joseph realizes that Mary his wife is pregnant, for the Bible says that she was found with child.

Joseph did not know at the time how Mary had gotten pregnant, but he did know it was not his baby. Note 1:19, that because Joseph was a just man, he was minded to put her away and not make her a public example. It sounds pretty serious to me. Back then one could be made a public example for this type of thing. Thus, Mary is pregnant and Joseph does not know how it happened, but it isn't his baby. Wouldn't you say, without knowing the real truth, that she had committed adultery? Maybe you would say, "No, because they were not married." Well, how about fornication? Fornication is a sex act between two unmarried people, which would seem to apply to this situation. So Joseph and Mary were engaged and were known to be husband and wife, according to Jewish law. Now Mary became pregnant during their engagement and it was not Joseph's baby. So it seems like Joseph would think that Mary had committed fornication during their engagement. Matthew 5:31-32 is the only place other than Matthew 19 where "for the cause of fornication is found." Note in Matthew 5:32, Jesus uses two words here that are very important: "saving for the cause of *fornication* and causes her to commit *adultery*."

Fornication and *adultery* are not the same. Otherwise Jesus would have said, "Saving for the cause of adultery." He didn't because *fornication* is sex when one is not married and *adultery* is breaking of marriage vows. So according to Jewish law, Jesus said that you could divorce your wife —engaged wife -- and divorce her according to Jewish law. Thus, Jesus was saying you could divorce your engaged wife. Divorce was permissible during the engaged state; but if divorce took place once married, it was adultery.

I do not intend to toss out a stumbling block or to condemn anyone. I am only allowed to proclaim the Word of God as I believe it in truth. Romans 7:2-3 gives a good explanation of marriage and divorce. Other scriptures in the New Testament regarding this matter on divorce and remarriage will be I Corinthians 7:2: "Nevertheless, to avoid fornication, let every man have his own wife, and let every woman have her own husband." Note the word **own** here. We are not to have what would be someone else's husband or wife, which would have once been married and divorced and remarried. I do not believe that anyone who marries lawfully should have a previously married living companion, an ex-husband or ex-wife. The Word of God testifies to this truth. Marriage is "until death do us part." It is not "Until fornication or adultery do us part." Other scripture regarding one husband or wife are I Timothy 3:2, "the husband of one wife"; I Timothy 3:12, "husband of one wife"; and Titus 1:16, "husband of one wife."

The New Testament tells us that there are three acts of adultery, not just one. Matthew 5:27-28: "Jesus said: ye have heard that it was said by them of old time, thou shalt not commit adultery: but I say unto you that whosoever looketh on a woman to lust after her hath committed adultery with her already in his heart. Then, in John 8:4 a woman was brought to Jesus who was caught in the very act of adultery.

If one divorces and remarries another, Jesus said, this is also adultery. Read Mark 10:11-12, Luke 16:18, and also Romans 7:2-3: "For the woman which hath an husband is bound by the law to her husband so long as he liveth; but if the husband be dead, she is loosed from the law of her husband. So then if, while her husband liveth, she be married to another man, she shall be called an adulterous; but if her husband be dead, she is free from that law; so that she is no adulteress, though she be married to another man."

The Word of God gives us a clear meaning when it comes to divorce and remarriage. This I know is a tough saying to mankind. The part of the wedding vow that says, "Til death do you part" is the only lawful way that one is lawfully married. If more people would read this and believe it, then marriage would not be taken so lightly.

In Matthew 12:39, Matthew 16:4, and Mark 8:38, Jesus refers to those times as an adulterous generation. This would testify to his words on divorce and remarriage. There are other scriptures throughout the New Testament that will testify to this belief of the scriptures.

There must have been those in the church then that were in this state of marriage. I Timothy 3:2: "A bishop then must be blameless, the husband of one wife." So here the church leaders, bishop and deacons, were not allowed to have more than one living wife. Also Titus 1:6 refers to one wife. I Corinthians 7:2 gives instruction for a husband to have his own wife.

There are only two options if one does divorce. According to I Corinthians 7:10: remain unmarried or be reconciled to one's own mate. So the Bible has much to instruct on this matter for those who may not quite understand. Again, I do not intend on tossing out a snare, but let everyone be fully persuaded in his or her own mind.

Stones

Stones have long been a part of the Old and New Testaments as well. Though I have no proof of it, I do believe the stone was first used by Cain to kill Abel. I believe this because of the long time use of the stone by Israel and God. The commandments that God gave Moses were engraved on tables of stone and could not be altered. In Exodus 24:12 God gave Moses the tables of stone, containing the law and the commandments that He had written. The stones were given as a thing for death. In Leviticus 20:2 the stone seemed to be used as a form of final judgment against one who broke God's law or commands. We see this being done in the New Testament in John 8:3-5 with the Pharisees and scribes, who were the religious leaders of that time. So we see that the stone was used by man to fulfill the law if it were broken.

In Matthew 3:7-9, John the Baptist here sees the Pharisees and the Sadducees coming to his baptism and gives them a stern warning. But look what John tells them in Matthew 3:9: "And think not to say within yourselves, we have Abraham to our father: for I say unto you, that God is able of these stones to raise up children unto Abraham."

Who are these children of the stones that are Abraham's? These are Abraham's children that had been stoned to death, and John said that God is able to raise them up. He will in the last day, the Word says.

At various times the Jews would try to stone Jesus, but the Word says they could not or did not as Jesus hid Himself and went out through the midst of them. This is recorded in John 8:59, John 10:31, and 10:39. It says that Jesus escaped out of the Jews' hands. Now in John 8:3-11, we have the story of the woman that was taken in the very act of adultery and was brought to Jesus to see what He would do. The Jews were told by Moses to put one to death by stones for breaking the law. But it says here also that the stones were unable to do their job. Well, we might say that all these events of the stones had reasons why the stoning was not done. This is man's understanding according to what they saw. I see things much differently than this. The stones of the earth were given a job to do in keeping or fulfilling God's law. You see Jesus said that He Himself, came to fulfill the law. Well, the stones were already doing this through condemnation by man and then death by the stones. So you could say that the stones had this job to do when it came to keeping God's law.

Well, now Jesus comes and He is the Rock, which is far Greater--bigger than the stone. Jesus' job is now to fulfill the law of God through forgiveness, mercy, and grace. You see that even the stones knew that Jesus was God, for in Luke 19:37-40 Jesus enters the city on an ass and the people rejoice. Now the Pharisees tell Jesus to rebuke his disciples. In Luke 19:40 Jesus told them: "And he answered and said unto them, I tell you, that, if these should hold their peace, the stones would immediately cry out." Now why would stones cry out when they can't talk? These stones would have. These stones knew Jesus and His job of fulfilling the law, so they knew they would not longer be asked to fulfill the law through death. The stones did not even like this job they were given. I also believe that the reason that Jesus could not be stoned is because the stones would not do this. This is why Jesus had to be crucified on the cross.

When Pilate said that he found no fault in Jesus, he told the Jews. John 18:31: "Take ye him and judge him according to your law. Look what the Jews say: the Jews therefore said unto him, it is not lawful for us to put any man to death that the saying of Jesus might be fulfilled, which he spake, signifying what death he should die." In John 19:6-7, Pilate says: "Take him, and crucify him for I find no fault in him. The Jews answered him, we have a law, and by or law, he ought to die, because he made himself the Son of God." The Jews knew that He should die, but they also knew that they could not kill Him. They had tried at various times and could not stone Him, which is the method the law stated was how they should kill Him for what He had done. The Jews were here smart enough to know that they, by their execution method, could not, as the stones would not, kill Him. This is probably where the saying of "dumber than a box of rocks" comes from. To me it sounds logical.

Rich or Poor

Does God care if we are rich or poor? Many Christians believe it is proper to be wealthy. In my reading of the New Testament, I have found that there are more warnings about wealth as a Christian than there are warnings against drunkenness. Now in the Old Testament wealth was a definite sign to the Jews. Abraham was wealthy; the Jewish priests were wealthy men also. Yes, wealth did have its place in the Old Testament, and it seemed to be a sign to the Jews that the person was really of God. I often believe that Jesus, whom the Jews recognized as a prophet had this recognition problem with the Jews. Look how many times the Jews said to Jesus, "Show us a sign from heaven." This always seemed to come after Jesus had done a miracle or done something great. Apparently the Jews did not recognize the miracles that Jesus did, even though Jesus had said: "If you don't believe my words, then believe me for the miracles that I do." But this was not good enough for they wanted that sign from heaven. Because Jesus had been called a priest and a king, this was the sign the Jews wanted to see from Him.

Well, who are Christians supposed to be following? The world? No, wealth is the world's standard for success. The pastor? No, he is to instruct us in the ways of righteousness and to help us keep on the straight and narrow. How about Jesus? Yes. Ephesians 4:13: "Till we all come in the unity of the faith, and of the knowledge of the Son of God, unto a perfect man, unto the measure of the stature of the fullness of Christ." So Jesus is the One we are to be like in all ways. Right? Let's look then at Jesus' life and His standard of wealth.

The Word says as a babe He was born in a manger, wrapped in swaddling clothes (Luke 2:7). In Luke 2:22-24 Jesus' parents offered a pair of turtle doves for an offering. A pair of turtle doves or two young pigeons was required in the law the not so wealthy person (Leviticus 5:7). Therefore, Jesus comes from a poor family. In John 1:29 and John 1:36, John the Baptist refers to Jesus as the Lamb of God. In Leviticus 4:27-32 it tells the sin offerings for the common man. The lamb is the sacrifice for the common man of that day.

Matthew 3:16 and Mark 1:10 give us record that John the Baptist, after or during Jesus' baptism, saw the Holy Spirit descend upon Jesus as a dove, in the form of a dove, as it was noticeable to him and was given to John as a sign from God about Jesus. The dove is a sacrifice for the poor in the Old Testament (Leviticus 5:7). This dove's descending upon Jesus is referred to in Luke 4:16-19. Jesus said that he had been anointed to preach the gospel unto the poor, where before the poor had been exempt. So this sign of the dove, a poor offering, was Jesus' anointing to preach the gospel to the poor of that time. Jesus had no house; the gospel records in Matthew 8:20 and Luke 9:58. "The Son of man hath not where to lay his head." Jesus did very much traveling while on earth and did not ride a horse or have a horse and buggy. All of Jesus' travels were on foot. When He did need an ass, then one was provided (Matthew 21:1-7).

Jesus never owned a boat either, but one was supplied when He needed it also.

What about money? Did Jesus have any money? The scriptures record that Jesus had money and a money manager, named Judas Iscariot. It was Judas' job to take care of the money. But Judas was a thief (John 12:4-6). If Jesus had no house, no boat, no horse, no donkey, but had money, what did He do with the money? According to scripture, Jesus used His money in three ways. John 13:26-29 tells us of the two things Jesus would do with His money. His disciples tell of buying what they needed and giving money to the poor. Matthew 17:24-27 tells us that Jesus also believed in paying taxes, which Peter did by following Jesus' word. I like to call tax money (what we pay our taxes with) fish mouth money. This is how Jesus paid His taxes. Jesus could certainly not be called a high roller, king, or a priest according to the world's standards.

The one thing that Jesus did own (recorded to be the very best) was His garments. John 19:23-24 gives us an idea of the quality of His vesture that He was wearing at the time they crucified Him. God doesn't really care whether we are well-to-do or are just getting by. The Bible does, however, tell us we are to be content. Philippians 4:11, Hebrews 13:5, and I Timothy 6:8: "With food and clothing therewith be content." God is more pleased with us to be common or equal when it comes to money. I am not condemning wealth, but believe that as Christians we will have far more difficulty being this way. "To whom much is given, much is required; and to whom little is given, little is required."

I cannot help but believe that there are far more things we will be required to do, if we have a lot of money. Much more than if we have very little money. I do not need the problems that wealth can bring. As a believer, I know that once my needs are met, I should help others who are in need.

Wouldn't it be wonderful if it really did work this way in our world today? This would be as close to being equal as you could probably get.

OUR LIVES, WHY?

When God created Adam and Eve, they were to live forever in the form they had been made. Of course, once sin entered, everything changed for the worst. Man's image was created in God's image and likeness, and we know God's image is incorruptible, immortal, and sinless. No sin would have given us God's image, in which we were created. Once Adam and Eve sinned, then their lives were put on a stop watch. They were then made subject to time and no longer had immortality. So now time becomes very relevant and man's life span is based on the time element.

Once Adam sinned, God could have said, "That's it. No more." But God did not. Rather, He limited life, which He had given, to time. God in His infinite mercy gave us another chance to become immortal. Only God has the exclusive rights on life, and says who can have it. He is Life and the Giver of it. God, seeing man's need, gives him what is a now a measure of precious life. Many people have their own idea of what and why we are still doing here. Most all ministers of the Gospel will say that the provision for our eternal life was first mentioned in Genesis 3:15. So God again gives man life even after man messes up.

The lifespan from Adam until now has changed from roughly a thousand years down to between seventy to ninety years. How we use this given time will determine where we wind up in eternity. There are two places we can spend eternity spoken of in the Bible. Of course, most people say they want to go to Heaven. The other place is Hell. The Word says that Hell was created for the devil and his angels and was not really intended for man. Matthew 25:41 tells us why hell was created. It was not created for man. So if man goes there, he will be out of place. Thus, there are two places to spend eternity and no in between. If you miss heaven, then you will wind up in hell.

Once man is given a measure of life from God, then his stop watch starts. The time in between is vital to our eternal destiny. Many people are given vast amounts of money in their lifetime, and some spend it wisely and others squander it. Life is often spent in much the same way as money. Both have limits and both are temporal. Well, God gives man this life, first and foremost in order to find eternal life through Jesus Christ our Lord. Then we are called to good works for the rest of our days. This is why we are given this life.

Now you must realize that Satan will attack you. The world has its standards when it comes to human life, and they sure do not go along with the Lord's plan. You see Jesus said He had overcome the world. The standards the world places on us are not God's standards, by no means. The world says you should be successful by fame, wealth, and education for all this success. And most mothers and fathers want to see their children do well in this world so they try to help their children achieve these standards. It helps to get through this world much easier. I completely understand this. I help my own children when I am able. But more than this I pray for my family's salvation and keeping. I know that everything here on earth will end one day. What we have will go to someone else after we leave this world. So I would much rather see my family's salvation more than anything else. I believe that once my family members accept Jesus, then my Lord is with them and will not leave or forsake them. Oh it may not be the best life by the world's standards, but it will be great by God's standards. I believe that once the Lord and accepted and followed that God's Word will change our minds and desire of our hearts.

I have heard the saying that a person is so heavenly minded that they are no worldly good. This is likely the way the world would look at a Christian who is living for the Lord. However, I am so thankful that God is the final judge in all matters. I Timothy 2:4: "Who will have all men to be saved, and to come unto the knowledge of the truth." This verse tells me we have been given life in order to find eternal life. Let's not waste it, please!

Serving Our Lord

While my wife and I were visiting some friends in Norfolk, Virginia, something happened to make me think spiritually. During New Years, my wife Carol and I teamed up with a family we came to know in Michigan in the 70's when I was saved. The pastor, under whose ministry I accepted Jesus, was there. We all stayed at his daughter's home. This was a special time because it is often difficult to find a group of people willing to discuss the Word of God and to learn from it. I had the opportunity to hear a young Navy chaplain speak on the Word of God. He told us of his duties with the military men and asked for our prayers to help him do the job he had been called to do. Our country seems to be moving farther away from the moral values that it once had. This man's job became increasingly more difficult with this issue. He said he deals with all denominations and faiths. He has had to learn to accept what others believe, which is the hardest part of the job.

During his time speaking about how things have become in our nation and how our country is moving away from the Word of God, I realized how many people have little or no belief in what the Bible says, especially about moral issues.

After he spoke, we were able to talk and ask questions. He believed the changes in the country started back in the 70's when the Bible and prayer were taken out of the schools. Things have continued to get worse ever since.

I have also observed a dramatic change in Jesus preaching churches. For example, in the church my wife attended in Greenville, SC, which had eight thousand members and was still growing, I noticed that there were vast numbers of people and quite a few young people responding to the altar call. Many of those who were at the altar had been there before and some had been there more than once. Why were so many returning to the altars? I connected the answer to the chaplain's speech. I asked Rick, my former pastor, why so many people were asking forgiveness time and time again? Why do we have such a rapid decline in our morals?

My brother-in-law has repeatedly told me he doesn't understand why his older brother and his brother's wife are back in the world. They had accepted Christ and had actually spoken in tongues, yet now they are in the world and their experience did not last very long at all.

That night I couldn't sleep for thinking about all I had heard and seen and how they were somehow connected. The Lord showed me what was going on because He knew I had asked Him in my heart for an answer to all this. When a person is given the knowledge of Jesus, it is the story of His great love and what He has done and how we need to accept Him, then he is at a point to make a decision to accept Jesus. Some churches explain the plan of salvation and tell the unsaved person he must repent. Well, what is *repent*? According to *Strongs* #3340 it means "To think differently or afterwards reconsider—feel compunction— repent." This word comes from the Greek #3339 which says: "to transform, change, transfigure." Unfortunately, not all salvation messages tell the person about repentance.

Jesus says in Luke 14:28, "For which of you, intending to build a tower, sitteth not down first, and counteth the cost?" Too many times a person is not given the price or cost of believing, and so many go back when something happens in their lives.

It is a common practice today for people not to be told the cost. For example, this is probably why so many people have houses and possessions repossessed. Maybe it is sometimes because of greed and deceit as well. At other times, there is small print on the contract and the person doesn't understand the real cost/price. So it is with a number of people. Thousands are led to Christ each year, and many do not realize what they are required to do as a Christian. Many will eventually go back to the world because there is no follow-up with them.

Acts 3:19 tells us, "Repent... and be converted." The message of Jesus was to repent and believe. If one does not repent when saved, then he or she will never go the pace. In the conversion process, one should repent at the very start. Repentance means that they should make a 180 degree turn in their thinking, especially regarding sin and how God thinks of sin. Repentance is the work of our faith. James 2:20 says, "Faith without works is dead." So if one believes in Christ, but he is not willing to repent, then his "faith is dead." If a newly saved person's way of thinking does not change, then neither will they. Many don't repent or aren't told of repentance, and they will soon return to the world from which they came. This is very sad indeed. If in the very beginning a person does not have this knowledge, then he doesn't make a proper decision. Our world today does not and will not change its way of thinking. The "god of this world hath blinded the minds of them which believe not" II Corinthians 4:4. Christians should work twice as hard because Satan is working overtime, knowing his time is short.

Many churches are not feeding and properly bringing up the children (newly saved people). Regardless of what one might do to prevent it from happening, not all of them will continue to follow after Christ and some will return to old ways. New believers should grow spiritually, "As newborn babes, desire the sincere milk of the word, that ye may grow thereby" I Peter 2:2.

We must help those to change their old desires to the new creature that they have become. I know this takes a gift from God to do properly. It depends a lot on teachers and not just anyone can properly teach. The Lord has changed my thinking from the world to the Lord by His Word. To me nothing else in the world or out of this world could have changed my thinking. After reading continually day to day the New Testament from beginning to end, year after year, the Word started working in me and my mind. Then I began to change the way I thought and the way I acted.

We take military men and put them through a training process first before using them in the military. We get them to think and act as military personnel. Not all can handle the military training and thus drop out. Although becoming a believer and a soldier are very different, they both take a change of one's mindset. If one does not change his thinking, then he will never become what is expected. The devil also knows that he mind controls the body and works with that thought in mind. Therefore, once a person has truly repented, then the conversion process begins and always continues as long as they continue to follow the Lord. Change is a requirement.

Change is something God has put into creation. The seasons, day and night, everything moves and everything changes. So God is an expert at change; His Word is an agent of change. Though the Word never changes, the Word is constantly changing us. The Word is the answer for everything that man can imagine here in this world. The Word is eternal.

Repentance definitely needs to be brought into the plan of salvation so that a person can make a proper decision. Many, though, will leave out repentance to get a high number of people to make a profession. They will lose these people later. Please give unbelievers the chance to weigh the cost!

RULE AND REIGN

There have been so many times I have heard, "I want Jesus to rule and reign in my life." We all as Christians would so very much want Jesus as our Lord to rule and reign in our lives. At one point in my walk with the Lord I have thought about ruling and reigning, and probably more than once. We often find this is not truly happening in our lives.

In order for Jesus to reign in our lives, we must first know the rules and keep them. You may say, "What do you mean?" Jesus is a king and anyone that knows anything about a king's kingdom knows that not everyone's laws or beliefs exist in a kingdom. Only one person is supreme and recognized in authority and that is the king alone. Everyone else's rules and beliefs, unless they line up with the king's, do not wash is his kingdom. I believe that this was and has been adopted by God so that there is and will not be any other laws or rules other than the King's Himself.

You may say, "Well, that sounds to be very dominating to a person," but I see it much more in the sense that there will be no mistakes or errors made here. Jesus tells us if we love Him, we are to keep His commandments. So to them that may not know Him or love Him, then His commandments have no or little influence on them. We see most of all this in their lifestyle. A person, even if not saved, is smart enough to know when one is living for and serving His Lord. As I have said before, God's Word is found unfit, for their way of life, so they do not honor it. Well, Jesus will one day rule and reign here on earth for a thousand years. Any that may still be here on earth after the rapture of the saints may have a problem with that, but so be it. We are told by God's Word that Jesus will return to earth one day with His saints to set up His kingdom of God here on this earth to rule and reign for a thousand years.

Well, why for a thousand years? In II Peter 3:8, Peter tells us: "But, beloved, be not ignorant of this one thing, that one day is with the Lord as a thousand years, and a thousand years as one day." So knowing this we see that the thousand years that Jesus will rule and reign here on earth as only two days on God's time table. I believe that one thousand year rule and reign will be the last day of this world. Prior to this last thousand years, one will find if he or she check sit out that the time from Adam until then will have been 6,000 years or 6 days with God. God is consistent and very well-organized in what He does.

Now along with this I have come across something else here with the 1000 years. I Corinthians 15:24-26 tells us that it is going to take that thousand years for Christ to put all His enemies under His feet. At this time Satan will be locked up so as not to deceive the world and still it will take 1000 years. Revelations 20:2-3 tells us what will happen to the devil during the thousand year reign of Christ. So little did I realize how many enemies my Lord and we Christians have. It is going to take a thousand years to put them down, so again I am getting a jump start by reading the New Testament time and gain, so I can get my Lord's rules down pat.

Forgiveness

Within the last year I have attended a couple of churches that had Sunday messages on forgiveness. Both pastors gave basically the same message on forgiveness. They said that we are to forgive others regardless of what was done or we would not be forgiven. God started to deal with me on forgiveness to others about four years ago. What the Lord was showing me is not a popular belief in most churches today.

When the Lord is speaking about forgiving others of trespasses, there are two different words that enter into play. The one Greek word is *ham-ar-ta-no* and the other word is *par-ap-to-mah*. In Matthew 6:15 and Matthew 18:35 these verses both pertain to *par-ap-to-mah*, which is number 3900 in *Strong's Concordance*. *Par-ap-to-mah* means "a side slip, lapse, or deviation i.e. unintentional error." This is not talking about one that steals, kills, or breaks other laws of our land. This word tells us that if a brother does something unintentionally to us then we are to forgive him or else we won't be forgiven. Now in Matthew 18:15, Luke 17:3-4, the words in these verses mean: "to miss the mark (and so not share in the prize), to sin" (#264, *Strongs*). This word means a major sin of man, which takes in the unlawful crimes of the land. In Luke 17:3 Jesus says: "If thy brother trespass against thee, rebuke him; and if he repent, forgive him." This word means "to miss the mark, trespass" (#264). Well, what if he does not repent for his trespass, then what? In Matthew 15:16-17 Jesus tells us the process that should be taken if one does not repent of sin against another. This *hamartano* sin is to be repented of or else. Jesus says that the person that committed the sin is to be considered a heathen man and a publican. There is no mention of forgiveness if the person committing the sin if they do not repent. This is not my own made-up understanding, but it comes from God's Word.

One may say, "Well, I am going to forgive anyway." Well, you can if you feel that way about it. And some will say that Jesus forgave the centurions who nailed Him to the cross and they didn't repent. Luke 23:33-34, "And when they were come to the place, which is called Calvary, there they crucified him, and the malefactors, one on the right hand, and the other on the left. Then said Jesus, 'Father, forgive them, for they know not what they do.' And they parted his raiment, and cast lots." In Luke 23:47, "Now when the centurion saw what was done, he glorified God, saying, 'Certainly this was a righteous man.'" You see before Jesus died, He asked for forgiveness for these men, though at that time they had not repented but rather performed the act of crucifying our Lord. You see in verse 47 where these same men now realize that they had done wrong for they realized Jesus was a righteous man. This to me seemed to be a man that was repenting as I am sure he had changed his mind on what he had just done in crucifying Jesus.

I had a pastor in the Detroit airport tell me that I needed to leave this doctrine alone. But I do not walk away from or leave alone anything that God reveals to me. Too many people are hiding the truth of God's Word when sometimes they know better. I do not believe God shows us something in His word only to have us not say anything to anyone else about it. Jesus said in Matthew 10:24: "The disciple is not above his master, nor the servant above his lord." So we know that when we come to the Lord for our salvation that we must ask Him to come into our lives and repent of our sins that Jesus has forgiven.

Now what happens if we would not repent? If we continue in sin, then would Jesus still forgive us? I myself do not believe that one would be forgiven if he or she returned back to the same sins that he or she had just been forgiven for. If we say that, we need to forgive even if one does not repent of their sin toward us. Then we must say that all people are forgiven of their sins even if they do not ask or repent. Think about it. We are not supposed to be above our Lord Jesus. Jesus will not and does not forgive sin if one does not ask for forgiveness of that sin and does not repent of it. We as Christians are to be loving and forgiving as Jesus is our example in this. At the same time we are to follow Jesus when we live our lives day by day. I believe that Love is unconditional, but forgiveness is conditional. The one condition is repentance of sin. One may call me wrong, but according to God's Word I believe I am right.

FEW AND MANY

The New Testament often refers to large numbers of people, but it doesn't give an accurate count. In Matthew 14:15-21 where Jesus feeds the multitudes, we see that this was 5,000 men, besides women and children. In Matthew 15:38, we are told that there are 4,000 men besides women and children. So, we see that a multitude is a large group of people and that they numbered four and five thousand besides women and children. Matthew 22:14: "For many are called, but few are chosen." Matthew 7:14: "Because strait is the gate, and narrow is the way, which leadeth unto life, and few there be that find it."

Because the New Testament doesn't give an accurate number when referring to man, I was wondering how many people are referred to by "few" and "many." Could the Bible be talking about hundreds, thousands, millions, what? For a long while, God did not see fit to give me a clear answer as to how many He means. I thought about the multitudes that followed Jesus, numbering 5,000 plus women and children at the most. In Acts 1:15, "And in those days Peter stood up in the midst of the disciples, and said, (the number of names together here were about 120.)" With this in mind,

I felt that I had something to work with that may give me some kind of an idea what my Lord meant by "few" and "many." Though I knew that what I would come up with would not be totally accurate or precise, but it would still give me an idea of the meaning of "few" and "many." Many times this is used throughout the New Testament with no real number given.

I took the number of disciples left on Pentecost, who would have been part of the 5,000 that followed Jesus, right? Well, though not an accurate number, I still claimed it for my use. After this I took the 5,000 followers of Jesus (though not completely accurate) and used it. So I had 120 out of 5000. After reducing this fraction, I got 3/125. I believe this number is close to the numbers God means with "few" and "many." "Few" equals 3 and "many" equals 125.

"Many are called, but few are chosen." Food for thought!

LIFE AND DEATH

The Bible makes it very clear to us about death and when one is dead. I Kings 17:17 says, "There was no breath left in them." Without breath there is no life. Once a person takes his last breath, then they are known as dead, having no life. Few people would disagree with this; it is common knowledge.

What about life then? When is a person first alive? Is it when the heart starts beating in the infant when it is yet in the womb? Is it when one first feels movement in the belly while carrying a child? What does the Bible say about when life begins in an infant? Gen 1:26-27 says, "And God said, 'Let us make man in our image, after our likeness: and let them have dominion over the fish of the sea, and over the fowl of the air, and over the cattle, and over all the earth, and over every creeping thing that creepeth upon the earth.' So God created man in his own image, in the image of God created he him; male and female created he them. In these verses God first creates. In Gen. 2:7 God then forms "man of the dust of the ground, AND BREATHED into his nostrils the breath of life; and man became a LIVING soul." So first God created man, and then He formed man.

Then He breathed into his nostrils the breath of life. Only after God gave man breath by breathing into his nostrils did he become alive, a living soul. So though there are many ideas regarding the beginning of life, the Bible only gives us one example.

I do not deny that a baby's moving in the womb and a heartbeat that can be detected are not a form of life, but not life as we know it. When the child is in the womb, it is being formed, the same as when God formed Adam. I believe it might have taken God nine months to form Adam. I believe this because my God is consistent, not erratic, and does keep and make everything in perfect order. Because God does not change, then His ways are forever. While the baby is in the mother's womb, being formed, I have been told the blood supply this is in the child will flow backwards in its body. Once the child is born, the blood will then flow in normal order through its body from then on. Once the child leaves the womb every effort is made to make sure that this child starts to breathe air. Now if the child starts to breathe, then it becomes a living soul as the word says. What if the baby does not take that first breath? If doctors are unable to get the infant to breathe, then we know that it will not normally survive and will soon be pronounced dead if it doesn't start to breathe.

Let me make it clear that I do NOT believe in abortion at all. Taking an infant from the womb before birth, before the child is ready, is wrong. Though our beliefs may vary on when life begins, the Word states when God breathed into the nostrils, and ONLY then does life begin. God is still the same and breathes into the newborn's nostrils. God's Word says He does not change.

THE BLOOD

Why did God choose the blood which runs through the veins of man's body to be a prime factor in our salvation? The blood is used as a proof of genealogy when we want to know where we came from and this normally will also let us know a lot about our ancestry. Not only does the blood prove family history, but also it will tell the doctors somewhat about what we might have in store have when it comes to problems that we may concur in our lifetime. This word man will call *genetics*, which merely means that if someone such as your mother or dad or grandparents had any health issues, then you could very well also wind up with them. Why? What is it about family history when it comes to our health and what we may be in store for in our lifetime? Leviticus 17:11 says, "For the life of the flesh is in the blood."

Now I believe that this scripture has manifold meaning; it talks of life. You see and know that without the blood in our bodies there could be no life in the body. Right? Well, I believe that the blood also determines how long the flesh can live. What I mean by that is that if there are hereditary diseases in your family history then those will show up sometime in your life and may very well shorten the length of your life here on earth. There are numerous things such as heart problems, diabetes, even cancer and many, many more than can be inherited. Why? Why do we have to accept these things in us that occurred in the past history of our family members? I believe that when Adam sinned that that sin went directly into the blood and was passed down to all men and women from that day forward to all of mankind.

I often ask people, "If Adam sinned and died, why do I have to die because Adam sinned?" Paul says, in Romans 5:14: "Nevertheless death reigned from Adam to Moses, even over them that had not sinned after the similitude of Adam's transgression, who is the figure of him that was to come." The reason that we die also is that when Adam sinned, that sin, which was not repented of, went into Adam's bloodstream and became hereditary to all of mankind from then on. Even human logic will tell you that this is true. The Word tells us that sin is paid to us in the form of a wage, as something that is earned. Romans 6:23: "For the wages of sin is death." We all know that at the end of a work week, or two, then we receive our paycheck which is the product of our wages that we receive for doing our job. So the payback for sin is the paycheck death. Not only is the physical death but can also be spiritual death after this life. Once there is enough compiled sin in our blood, I believe that death will come. I believe that this sin from our ancestors also which is in the blood will also stake its claim on our lives. This to me is the only logical answer that I can come up with when there is premature death in a person. We do not know why they are taken so early in life, whether by disease or accident, but we know that it does happen.

I do not completely understand why God places or allows unrepented sin to enter into the bloodstream of our bodies, but I believe that it does. You see that before Adam sinned there was no physical death, so Adam would have lived forever had he not have sinned. With this sin, as well as others that occur in our lives, they all enter into our blood to give us the wage of physical death to our bodies. Once God speaks something it is so and cannot be changed. But God knew that the physical death was unavoidable in this life, because "it is appointed unto man once to die, after that the judgment." Not only the physical death came from Adam's sin, but the spiritual death also which would have made man non-existing as we would have all, after physical death, then perished. Thanks be to God He gave mankind a second chance, though he did not deserve it, and sent Jesus, His only begotten Son, to pay the price for all of mankind. Man does not have to suffer the second death, which comes after this physical life, if we find Jesus Christ as our Lord and Savior sometime in this life we are given by God.

God is so good! He gives us physical life after Adam's sin, only a measure though, and gives us eternal life, which Adam lost, through and by His Son, Jesus Christ. Jesus paid the debt for our sins so now through Him and what He did on the cross and being resurrected, we can have eternal life. This was lost to sin in the first man, Adam, and then offered back to mankind through and by Jesus. Thank you so much my God! Praise you!

So we see that sin enters the blood, unrepented sin, and causes death sooner or later. So the length of life we live depends on our blood we have in our veins.

Man has taken and used drugs to try and ease the effects of this sin, but this can only postpone the inevitable for a short while at its best. I told my doctor, who is a believer in Jesus, that drugs are man's way of coping with the sins he has committed in life. My doctor agreed with this statement. Another scripture that bears witness to what I believe is St. John 9:2: "Who did sin, this man, or his parents, that he should be born blind?" Even the disciples knew that the illnesses of man came from sins; even though this blindness was to glorify God. So if unrepented sin goes in the blood and causes death to mankind, then what takes it away? Well, not the physical death but the spiritual death is taken from us through and by the blood of Jesus. His blood had no sin in it. The Word tells us His blood was the only price that God would accept for our salvation. So death comes from the blood but is taken away by the blood also. They say that extracting the blood from the body when one dies will help to prolong the flesh. So corruption occurs faster with the blood.

Also, I do not believe our new bodies will have blood in them. St. Luke 24:39 says, "Behold, my hands and my feet, that it is I myself: handle me, and see; for a spirit hath not flesh and bones, as ye see me have." Here flesh and bone is mentioned, but not blood. Also when Thomas put his finger and hands into Jesus' wounds I am sure that there was not any blood. This is found in John 20:27. Jesus had at that time the new body that we as believers will one day have also. Jesus said: "Because I live ye shall live also." I base my belief of no blood in our new bodies on the Word of God in I Corinthians 15:50. Here Paul says: "Now this I say, brethren, that flesh and blood cannot inherit the kingdom of God." So here there is no blood in the kingdom of God, but because of Luke 24:39, I do believe that flesh and bone can inherit the kingdom of God. I believe that the new bodies that we will receive in the resurrection are for the kingdom of God's use here on earth during the one thousand year reign with Christ and also in heaven when we enter there. All that I read in the Word of God leads me to believe this is so.

WHAT IS THE FOUNDATION OF GOD?

In Matthew 16:13, Jesus asks the question to his disciples: "Whom do men say that I the son of man am?" The disciples then give Him a variety of answers as to whom men say that He is. But Jesus wants to know who the disciples believe Him to be. In verse 16, Peter declares Jesus to be "the Christ, the Son of the living God." From here on out there are a couple of things which take place that I had never really seen before. Not only does Peter recognize Jesus, but in verses 17-18, Jesus recognizes Simon Peter and calls him by his names, Simon Barjona, Peter (18), and the name which Jesus gave him. In verses 15-18 we here see that both Jesus and Peter know each other by name. Now verse 18 is where many people may come up with different answers if they are given the question: What is the rock that Jesus is building His church upon? Most of the time many will answer, Jesus is the Rock. This is what He is building the church on and the gates of hell will not prevail against the church. Yes, at first glance this may well be what one sees, but I see these verses much differently than that. You see what Jesus is saying, and read along here with me, is that Peter knows Jesus as the Christ, and Jesus knows Peter as He calls him by both his names. When Jesus says thou art Peter and upon this rock I will build my church, He is saying that Peter knows Him and Jesus knows Peter and upon this rock, or foundation, **of knowing each other**, Jesus will build his church and the gates of hell will not prevail against Jesus knowing us and us knowing Jesus.

Want more proof on this? II Timothy 2:19 says: "Nevertheless the foundation of God standeth sure, having this seal, The Lord knoweth them that are his. And let everyone that nameth the name of Christ depart from iniquity." You see the foundation is the rock Jesus was talking about, a solid foundation where Jesus knows us and we Him. In Matthew 7:21-23 we see even more proof of this. In verse 22 the person is quoting the signs of a believer in Christ which are found in Mark 16:17-19: cast out devils, speak with new tongues, prophesy in thy name, and many wonderful works, all of which are done in the name of Jesus. Look at verse 23, where Jesus says: "I never knew you: depart from me, ye that work iniquity." In Luke 13:23-27, we see another scripture that bears witness to the vision that my Lord has given me on this also. John 10:1-5 tells of how Jesus knows His own sheep, and calls them by name (v.3).

You see, we must come to know Jesus and Who He is for our salvation; but it is not just enough for us to know Him, He must know us by name. The only way this happens is through a personal relationship with Jesus, as Lord, and our departing from iniquity, we that claim the name of Christ. We see in Luke 16:19-31 the story which Jesus tells of the rich man and Lazarus, which is a beggar. Both died and went to different places after death. But note how Jesus calls the beggar by his name of Lazarus; but the rich man, He does not call by name for He never knew him. Some other

NEW TESTAMENT REVELATIONS

scriptures which bear witness to this are I Corinthians 8:3 and also Galatians 4:9. This is the foundation of God and not even the gates of hell can prevail against us knowing our Lord Jesus and Jesus knowing us, His sheep, by name.

SIN AND ITS EFFECTS

I f I had to pick a time of the year that Adam and Eve sinned, it would be the month of October. Why? Is it really important? Yes, I believe it is, as anything that God reveals to us is important. I believe they sinned in October for a number of very good reasons. In Genesis 1:29, God gave Adam every herb bearing seed, and every tree in the garden which is the fruit of a tree yielding seed. So everything Adam ate for food came from trees or herbs of the ground. Everything grew from the ground that they ate to live. You see there was fruit on the trees and everything grew year round for them to eat. Not until after Noah had landed on land with his Ark did things change. Genesis 9:3, God tells Noah that now every moving thing that lives shall be meat now, even as the green herb had been also. Why? I believe that from that point on the seasons changed dramatically and that from then on there was a growing season and a season that was dead to growing, so the fruit would no longer be on the trees year round for them to eat. It was the sin of man that changed all of this and caused it to happen and nothing else. I believe at this point that sin caused the tilt of 23.5 to come about and from that point on the earth would have an elliptical, elongated orbit around the sun. This would give us the climate and temperature changes we experience now in our seasons.

We know that we plant in the spring, and we harvest in the fall, our growing season. If the fruit and vegetable are not harvested by the fall, then the fruit and vegetables will die and be of no use to us as it does not stay year round for us to eat. This is why God gave animals to man to eat so he might have food in the winter months to eat and not starve. October is known as the harvest month and many still use this saying instead of Halloween which also falls in October. Halloween is considered to be Satanic in nature to many and this is when the apple, which some believe Eve ate, is used for bobbing for apples and apple cider, a very popular thing around and during Halloween in October.

So October starts the change of our seasons and is called fall. The fall of man -- what a coincidence this is! This is the month that the leaves fall from the trees but just before this we have spectacular color from them. I love the fall for colors here in Michigan as it is a beautiful or should I say one of the most beautiful times of the year. Is it not like our God to take something bad and turn it into something beautiful for you? Also, October is the month God told the Jews to start to keep track of time, as October 10 is the Jewish New Year. Before Adam sinned there was no need of time as he and Eve would have lived forever. When Adam sinned, all of mankind was put on the stopwatch and became subject to time. Now instead of eternal life, Adam and man are given a measure of life which ends with time. This all comes from sin. Sin is the only thing I have seen that takes things out of the perfect order that God puts them in.

Science also bears witness to what I believe about the month of October as the sun moves around celestial equator on or close to a path called the ecliptic. The ecliptic orbit of the sun crosses the celestial equator of the earth at Autumn (autumnal) which is the northern hemisphere's fall. It also will cross again in the spring when the earth came out of its winter months. All of this now occurs because of the earth's tilt and elliptical orbit which changed because of man's sin, unrepented sin.

And if we look, we will see that with sin that man's lifespan changes. Adam was given almost a thousand years; and after Noah, man has 120 year maximum. You see with the sin the food changed to animals and the animals help to shorten our lifespan. Many say too much meat causes many problems in our life and can shorten it. Again, the wages of sin is death. I do believe that many of the rare things we are experiencing in our weather and other problems come from man's sin that he refuses to let go of and continues to do. His love of money is greater than anything else to him. Man's life-long goal or standard is success, wealth, financial security in this life and man will stop at nothing to obtain this, as he feels, with strong feelings, that this is right. So don't blame God for all the weird things that are happening, blame sin, as it causes it all to happen.

THE DOVE

In Matthew 3:16, Mark 1:10, Luke 3:22, and John 1:32, all of these record the baptism of Jesus by John the Baptist. This vision of the dove upon Jesus was seen by John, and John 1:32 says: "And John bare record, saying, I saw the Spirit descending from heaven like a dove, and it abode upon him [Jesus]." What significance could the symbol of the dove have on this event?

In Leviticus 5:7 we have a record where the Jews are told what should be the sin offerings for the poor, and it is two turtle doves. Also there are sin sacrifices for the rich, the leaders, and the very poor found here, but the one that is of interest is the dove. The dove was also used by Noah to find dry land after the flood in Gen. 8:8-12. So what is it I am getting at? Luke 4:16: "And he came to Nazareth, where he had been brought up; and as his custom was, he went into the synagogue on the sabbath day, and stood up for to read. And there was delivered unto him the book of the prophet Esaias. And when he had opened the book, he found the place where it was written, The Spirit of the Lord is upon me, because he hath anointed me to preach the gospel to the poor." Now this was after Jesus had been baptized, and John had seen the Spirit descending upon Jesus in the form of a dove. This I do believe was the anointing that Jesus received to preach the gospel unto the poor and was witnessed by John. The dove John saw was the symbol of the poor, as denoted in the Old Testament. Now I do not say this scripture could not have manifold meaning but I have only seen this one thing from it.

Blind

In John 9:39, Jesus is talking to the Pharisees, and says: "For judgment I am come into this world, that they which see not might see, and that they which see might be made blind." This He said, after He had healed a man who was born blind. Some of the Pharisees which heard Him asked saying in verse 40: "Are we blind also?" The Pharisees thought that they had heard Jesus speak of physical blindness to the eyes when He said this. Jesus always took the natural and used it to give a spiritual truth to those who were listening to Him. The first part of Jesus' statement, "that they which see not might see" was talking of the physical blindness of man, and Jesus did cure a few of them while on earth.

What about "that they which see might be made blind"? The Pharisees did not understand this part. They thought that Jesus was meant a person that could see physically would be made so that he could not see anymore, not realizing He meant them. Because the Pharisees were carnal in their thinking, they could not understand what Jesus meant. In Genesis 3:6-7, the woman ate of the forbidden tree and gave to her husband and the eyes of them both were opened and they knew that they were naked. Once they had disobeyed, sinned, they their eyes were opened because they now had sin. John 9:41: "Jesus said unto them, 'If ye were blind, ye should have no sin: but now ye say, We see, therefore your sin remaineth." So now we can spiritually see what Jesus was speaking of here. Will those Pharisees ever learn?

FOR THIS CAUSE

In Genesis 2:24, after Adam had been given his wife from God, it was said in verse 24: "Therefore shall a man leave his father and his mother, and shall cleave unto his wife: and they shall be one flesh." Here God said: a man shall leave father and mother once he finds a wife. At this point in time there were only Adam and his wife and there were no mothers or fathers, only after Adam and Eve had children. This Word of God may well be why we see such a bonding that exists in the daughters toward their mothers even after they get married. In my lifetime I have seen very few men that have this close, close relationship with their parents. I know that as children we are to honor our parents and help to take care of them if needed. I see much more than this relationship though when it comes to the daughter even after they are married to their husbands. "Why is it like this?" I used to ask myself, because it's not like that with the man. Well, dwelling upon God's Word, I believe I have found the answer to my question. Because God spoke this of the man, when he marries, finds a wife, this is why the man does not have a difficult time in leaving his father and mother for a wife. The woman, on the other hand, has to be given away by the father. I believe that that is the reason here for the father giving the daughter in marriage. Now it may not be all of the reason, but I believe that the custom definitely came from the fact of God's Word spoken over the man but never over the woman. This is more food for thought.

IVES

In the New Testament there are a couple of brothers: the **Ives** brothers. These two brothers are <u>red</u> in the book of Acts. Acts tells us that the one brother is more blessed than the other brother. But the brother that is less blessed is the one that most people admire or would like. Now when these two brothers are together they create a law of God. Give up? If you open your Bibles to Acts 20:35: "Remember the words of the Lord Jesus, how He said, It is more blessed to **give** than to rece**ive**." The words of our Lord here are normally in newer Bibles printed in red, so the brothers are red in the book of Acts. Ok?

THE FLESH AND BLOOD AND LIFE

John 6:53-54: "Then Jesus said unto them, Verily, Verily I say unto you, except ye eat the flesh of the Son of man, and drink his blood, ye have no life in you. Whoso eateth my flesh, and drinketh my blood, hath eternal life; and I will raise him up at the last day." This passage of scripture has been used by many churches as a communion scripture. The scripture talks of eating the flesh and drinking the blood of Jesus. Is this not what we do when we take communion? My belief on the scriptures regarding the blood and flesh of Jesus has a totally different meaning.

In Leviticus 26-27, the Jews are instructed by God to eat no blood at all, and then Jesus tells them that except they eat of the flesh of Him and drink His blood, they have no life. So what could Jesus be speaking of here? Was He talking of the communion with the blood and flesh? We use wine or grape juice for the blood and usually a special cracker or bread for the flesh symbol in communion. I believe that this is much more what Jesus is saying to us than communion. In I Corinthians 11:24-26 Paul speaks of the taking of communion: "For as often as ye eat this bread, and drink this cup, ye do shew the Lord's death till he come" (v.26). Well, here we are told that communion is the showing openly of the Lord's death till He returns. So the eating of the flesh and drinking of the blood that Jesus speaks of in John 6:53-54 is onto life and the taking of communion is recognizing the death of Jesus. Is this not what the scripture says? What do you suppose Jesus was speaking of then in John if it was not communion? Let me see if I can show you what I have been shown here. John 1:14: "And the word was made flesh, and dwelt among us." The Word of God, Jesus, was made flesh. Now in Matthew 26:28 Jesus says: "For this is my blood of the new testament…." So let me see: the Word of God was made flesh and Jesus' blood was of the New Testament. So could Jesus have been telling us that we need the Word of God in the New Testament in us, in our hearts, so we may have life in us? In John 6:63, which is after Jesus speaks of the flesh and blood, He says: "It is the spirit that quickeneth; [or gives life], the flesh profiteth nothing: the words that I speak unto you, they are spirit, and they are life."

Well? What do you think? IF Jesus' Words He speaks are spirit and the spirit is life, then could He not be saying to us that His Words of the New Testament must be in us by reading and using in our everyday of life to have life? I believe that this is exactly what my Lord is saying. I have said before the New Testament is my eternal life assurance policy. This may well be what Jesus was saying in deed.

I Go To Prepare a Place

The Word of God tells us that as a believer in the Lord Jesus Christ that we are saved and have our eternal home in heaven with Christ. John 14:2-3, Jesus says, "I go to prepare a place for you. And if I go and prepare a place for you, I will come again, and receive you unto myself: that where I am, there ye may be also." So after this life we are going to be with Jesus.

So what about this, "I go to prepare a place for you"? Many of us in today's world have attended concerts with rock or Christian performers. In order to get in the door at concert time we must possess a ticket for the concert. Now the ticket that we obtain at time of purchase will tell us where we sit during the concert, right? OK. So we are with our ticket and now have a location in the building where we can watch the concert. A very important thing, though, is that the seat that we will hold during the concert will be determined by the amount of money we are willing to pay for our ticket at the time of purchase. Get where I am coming from yet? Well, if we want a close and really good seat where we can see the performers well and also hear well, as most are very loud, then we must be willing to pay a little more or maybe a lot more money than you could get just a standard ticket for. I do not believe that this concept came from man. I believe that we are in the likeness of God our Father and that this came from Him. You see, though we as Christians have had a place for us in eternity, even before we were born, the place, as Jesus said, has yet not been prepared for us as we have not yet paid the full price for our tickets yet. As long as we are on this earth and in this body, we have got the time to pay on that place which has not yet been prepared for us. The more of the world we overcome and the closer we get in this life to Jesus and His Word, I believe that our place that will be prepared for us will be based on.

Jesus said the scribes liked to sit in Moses' seat, but not all will have Moses' seat in heaven. In Matthew 20:20-23, "Then came to him the mother of Zebedee's children with her sons, worshipping him, and desiring a certain thing of him….She saith unto him, Grant that these my two sons may sit, the one on thy right hand, and the other on the left, in thy kingdom." Jesus told her that it would be given to them for whom it was prepared and that was up to the Father and not Him. So that place, prepared by Jesus, for us in eternity, with Him, is still in the making as long as we are in this body here on earth. God felt that eternity was such an important place that everyone should have a home there, even the devil and his angels. The main thing regarding this in my thinking is what the Word says about it. He who is least shall be greatest here; and the last shall be first; and the first last. God is truly "not a Respecter of persons," and we cannot work our way to our place, but it can and will be in accordance to our faith we have toward Him and how we act on that faith we have toward or Lord Jesus Christ. We are called to good works as Christians and by this I believe we are recognized, but our faith pleases God, and Abraham was the father of that faith.

Food for thought, huh?

SENSES

We are told that as humans, we have the sense of hearing, seeing, tasting, smelling, and touching. Well, let me give you a new one. I believe that we as humans have three senses. What? We have a rich sense, poor sense, and right in the middle of these two, we have common sense. Now only one of these senses is God–given: common sense. The word "common" means "equal, not above and not below but common or equal." Now rich sense does not recognize or believe in poor sense as it only believes in rich sense and doesn't recognize poor sense. Rich sense really has very little common sense, if any, because rich sense only allows rich to run and rule his thinking and doing. Rich sense has its own way of doing things and does not believe that any other way will work, at least not as well as their way will or does. Below rich sense and on the opposite side of the track is poor sense. Poor sense recognizes rich sense, but does not understand it or how it may work, but just rather accepts it and moves on in its own realm of poor sense which it may not altogether really like, but does understand and accepts.

Now right in the middle of rich and poor sense, we have the God-given common sense that man has (at least most men anyway). Common sense is neither rich nor is it poor, but rather is equal or common; nor does it want to be rich or poor, but is quite happy being common or equal and does not seem to experience the problems that the rich or the poor may have. I believe that God wanted all men to be equal or common as this was the sense that we are given from birth and does help us cope with the problems of this world.

The rich, most of the time, will apply very little (if any) common sense to a problem because they do not seem to have much common sense. They had rather let rich sense rule and reign in their lives and problems of this life. I do find that most poor people do know and recognize common sense and can and do apply it much of the time to their lives and problems. The man that is common, though, seems to have the least amount of difficulty when it comes to the problems of this life we face. It seems that common sense works well on most of life's problems, at least or better than rich sense or poor sense might. So might it not be far better for man to be common rather than rich or poor as the two (aside from common) seem to have a whole different idea on the cares of this life. At least it seems that way to me.

More food for thought.

BEHOLD THE FIG TREE

In Matthew 21:17, it tells us where Jesus left the city of Jerusalem and went and lodged in a town called Bethany. "Now in the morning as He returned into the city, He hungered. And when He saw a fig tree in the way, He came to it and found nothing thereon, but leaves only, and said unto it, Let no fruit grow on thee henceforward forever. And presently the fig tree withered away. And when the disciples saw it, they marveled, saying, "How soon is the fig tree withered away!" (Matthew 21:18-20). Mark 11:12-14 and Mark 11:20-21 give us the same story, only a few things are a little different in it, giving us a little more meaning. We see in Mark it was noticed by the disciples the next day as they entered the city.

I have heard but some that this story is supposed to be about us as fruit bearers for Jesus. This may well or well not be, but I myself have received a different understanding of this story told to us. I believe that when Jesus approached the fig tree, He expected fruit to be on it as He was hungry. But the disciples knew that the time for figs had not yet come. But if the disciples knew, then why did not Jesus know? Before Adam sinned and even after that until the days of Noah there was fruit on the fruit trees year round. How do I know this? It says that after Noah had landed on dry land then God gave the animals over to him to be food. Why? Well because sins had caused a change in the earth's orbit and tilt angle so that the earth no longer had good weather year round, and we then had hot and cold and growing seasons for the fruit trees. Summer months would be for growing and fall for harvest and then animals would be for food in the winter months so as man would not starve. If you read about Noah and his escape from the flood, you will also see what I am telling you about the animals for food after the flood. So no longer was fruit on the trees year round, but only during the growing season.

Now when Jesus approached the fig tree I believe that He expected fruit to be on that tree as Jesus was without sin and the tree should have known that. In John 1:10 it says: "He was in the world, and the world was made by him, and the world knew Him not." So that tells me that the fig tree did not know Jesus. What a mistake that was! If not knowing Jesus could cause this to happen to a fig tree; then what about us? Can you see why it is so important to know Jesus? Jesus is our only source of life and without Him I do not believe that there is any life because He is the source of life itself. "He who hath the Son hath life and he who has not the Son has not life." Life comes through and by the Lord Jesus Christ only. Those that face eternity and do not know Jesus or will not accept Him have no hope for life, just like the fig tree that knew Jesus not.

WOMAN

The Word says that in the beginning God created all things. In His creations was man and woman on the sixth day. We see that man was formed from the dust of the earth. Genesis 2:7 says, "God formed man of the dust of the ground, and breathed into his nostrils the breath of life; and man became a living soul." Well, what about the woman? In Genesis 2:21-23, God caused a deep sleep to fall upon Adam and he slept. This is much like the hospitals do today and cause sleep through an anesthetic which is given to the person before surgery. After God causes a deep sleep on Adam, God takes a rib from Adam's side; and with that rib, he made a woman. We see that Adam and even the animals of the earth were formed from the dust of the earth, but the woman was the only thing made and not formed. She is now bone of Adam's bone and flesh of his flesh and so he calls her woman.

I have told my wife and others that because woman was made and not formed is probably the reason that they derive the name in the Bible as "maids." Now, I know the spelling is different, but it may well be that because of this that women are old maids, young maids, maidens, work maids. Come on, give it some thought. Could it not be this? I do not believe that this would be a subject of interest to the ladies at a woman's gathering though. In I Peter, he speaks of the wife as the weaker vessel and that we should honor her as such, so that our prayers are not hindered. I have been married for going on 44 years to the same lovely lady, and I love her dearly. One night at a Bible study with the brothers at a Baptist church, I was headed to the church parking lot after the study. My wife was not with me and was at home that night for some reason. On my way to my care one of the brothers said, "Going home, Lee?" I said, "Yes, Brother, I am headed home to the weaker vessel (meaning my wife)." This brought a smile to the brother's face, as he knew me well to be a not so serious guy at times. I was only giving honor where honor was due.

FORNICATION

It may be that the word *fornication* in the New Testament may have manifold meaning. *Fornication* is not only in the natural sense with man and woman, but is also used in spiritual fornication as well. The fornication in the natural between the man and woman is what I will discuss. The meaning of the word *fornication* has come to have new meaning today as it seems that man has changed its meaning today so as to fit the way he believes it to be.

The word *fornication* in the older Webster dictionary meant sex between two people, man and woman, who were not married. The word *fornication* used to mean sex outside the bounds of marriage. **Used to**. Today in dictionaries as well as the *Strong's Concordance*, it is used as an immoral sex act and does not distinguish between married or single people. The word *adultery* definitely means a sex act, illegally committed between two people, one of which is married. *Adultery* means, "The illegal or unlawful sex between two married or one married person, breaking of the marriage vows taken." *Adultery* pertains to only marriage; whereas man now says *fornication* can does mean either married or single. Thank God that His Word changes not to suit man and his deeds.

Matthew 5:32 and Matthew 19:9 are the only places in the New Testament that "for the cause of fornication" is used. Because Jesus uses it pertaining to husband and wife, most people take it to be married. A closer look and study will reveal that it does pertain to single, engaged, but not yet married, man and woman. This is shown when Joseph was going to put Mary away (divorce her) when he discovered she was pregnant and not yet married, just engaged. Under Jewish law, in order for them to separate, once engaged, they must get a divorce. Once married, however, it was "until death do you part." Nowhere have I ever heard in the marriage vows, "Till fornication (or adultery) do you part." Why? The Bible does not support divorce for fornication or adultery. Man has taken tradition and doctrines of man to make the word of God of no effect pertaining to divorce and re-marriage. Everything has been changed and taught to support what man wants and not what God says about divorce and remarriage.

In John 8:41 the Jews tell Jesus that they are not born of fornication but have one Father even God. So here it sounds as though the Jews believed that having more than one husband could well mean fornication. You see the Jews knew the true meaning of the word fornication in the day it was used in the Bible. In I Corinthians 7:2, Paul says, "Nevertheless, to avoid fornication, let every man have his own wife, and let every woman have her own husband" -- not someone else's. *Own* to me means something that is not someone else's but mine and mine alone. If a couple divorced and remarried, they would be someone else's wife or husband as long as their previous mate were still alive. If previously married and the ex is still alive, the Word says when they remarry someone else, they commit adultery against the previous mate. This explains why John the Baptist said that Herod's marriage to his brother's wife was unlawful, at least under God's law.

Also when Jesus said that this is a wicked and adulterous generation, back in the days He was on earth, tells me that what He was talking about was divorce and remarriage in that day. Jesus said on numerous occasions that if one divorced his/her mate and remarried that they were committing adultery. I do not think lots of people in that day were married and cheating on each other. For one thing, we see that such a deed, if and when one was caught, was punishable by death by stoning under Moses' law. We see this was still in practice when the woman who was caught in the very act of adultery was brought to Him. Jesus knew there was a difference in meaning when He used the two words, *fornication* and *adultery*, in the verses in Matthew. If they were the same, why did He use two different words? Even the Greek translation of the words is two totally different words, not only in speech but also in meaning. If one would take the time and do a study from the New Testament on marriage and divorce and see what the Word reveals to them, they would see it is far different than what the world and man teaches.

ONE SIZE FITS ALL

The Word of God is the only truth that I know of that exists in the world. Jesus said in John 17:17: "Thy word is truth." I Peter 1:25 says: "But the word of the Lord endureth forever," so the Word of God is truth and also eternal, lasting forever. Because God's Word is eternal, His judgments are eternal also. God's Word is absolute truth that comes in only one size, but the one size fits ALL.

What do I mean? Well, some people may try to stretch the Word of God a little to get it to fit their particular situation. Most people, though, will see when God's Word does not really fit. Some may try to downsize or shrink the Word of God by leaving some of it out, trying to get it to stand for what they claim to be right or proper doctrine. Some usually see by knowing the Word that this does not fit in properly either.

Some people will neither stretch the Word nor shrink the Word, but will rather not accept the Word of God as they find it to be unfit for their way of life that they have chosen to live. People should realize that God's Word was given to us to live by. Luke 4:4: "And Jesus answered him, saying, 'It is written, That man shall not live by bread alone, but by every word of God." So you could say that one size here does – or at least is supposed to – fit all.

New Bodies

The word *glory* in the New Testament can and does have numerous meanings, depending on how it is used. Jesus speaks in Luke 24:26 "Ought not Christ to have suffered these things, and to enter into his glory?" In Luke 9:28-32, Jesus is transfigured before Peter, James, and John, and is seen with Moses and Elias "who appeared in glory." Jesus also speaks of this appearance of Him, Elias, and Moses as being seen coming in His kingdom, Matthew 16:28.

Romans 3:23, "For all have sinned and come short of the glory of God." Well, Jesus when seen in His glory with Moses and Elias, who were dead physically, but here appeared alive with Jesus. When we sin, or I should say when Adam sinned, he gave up or came short of eternal life that he had before sinning. So once Adam sinned, he fell short of the eternal life that he once had; or shall we say the glory of God, because eternal life is only given and can only be taken by God Himself.

Jesus often spoke of his glory, which was after his physical life that He then had. Now when Jesus appeared in glory, or His new life, He must have also had a new body, for He was seen in his kingdom. Matthew 16:28. Paul says in I Corinthians 15:50, "Now this I say, brethren, that flesh and blood cannot inherit the kingdom of God." When Jesus was resurrected on the third day and was in his new body, appeared to the disciples in the house they were in. Now the disciples thought that he was a spirit but look what he says in Luke 24:39: "Behold my hands and my feet, that this is I myself: handle me and see; for a spirit hath not flesh and bones as ye see me have." So if Jesus was in his new body and this is the body of the kingdom of God, as corruption does not inherit incorruption, speaking of the bodies, we now have. So the new body is incorruptible meaning we will not rot or decay and is seen also in the kingdom of God Jesus said. Now the new body does not have or contain flesh and blood but does contain flesh and bone Jesus said. So the blood will be of no use in the new bodies. I have said that the blood of man contains the sin or sins of this life and stores these sins and passes them on to future generations which are called genetic by man. So my belief is that the new bodies we receive after we are resurrected will be for the kingdom of God, our eternal bodies as God had intended in Adam.

These bodies will be flesh and bone but not blood. This will then be the glory of God that man fell short of when Adam sinned. This was Adam's blood that was transmitted to all generations. So our eternal life is now restored through the second man Adam, Jesus through faith and confession.

It is marvelous what God has done for man through and by His own Son, Jesus Christ! Amen!